BEARS OF THE WORLD™

# POLAR BEARS

**DIANA STAR HELMER**

The Rosen Publishing Group's
**PowerKids Press**™
New York

*Many thanks to Don Middleton, member of the Great Bear Foundation, International Wildlife Rehabilitation Council, and founder and webmaster of The Bear Den, at http://www2.portage.net/~dmiddlet/bears/index.html.*

Published in 1997 by The Rosen Publishing Group, Inc.
29 East 21st Street, New York, NY 10010

First Edition

Book Design: Danielle Primiceri

Photo Credits: Cover shots © Mark Newman/International Stock, © Ronn Maratea/International Stock; p. 4 © Joanna McCarthy/Image Bank; p. 7 © Ron Maratea/International Stock; p. 8 © Joe Van Os/Image Bank; p. 11 © Scott Wm. Hanrahan/International Stock; p. 12 © AP/Wide World Photos; p. 15 © Bill Hickey/Image Bank; p. 16 © Ocean Images, Inc./Image Bank; p. 19 © Mark Newman/International Stock; p. 20 © Harald Sund/Image Bank.

Helmer, Diana Star, 1962–
    Polar bears /Diana Star Helmer.
    p.   cm. — (Bears of the world)
    Includes index.
    Summary: Provides a simple introduction to the physical characteristics, behavior, and habitat of polar bears.
    ISBN 0-8239-5130-8
    1. Polar bear—Juvenile literature. [1. Polar bear. 2. Bears.] I. Title. II. Series.
Ql737.C27H45 1996
599.786—dc21

96-47207
CIP
AC

Manufactured in the United States of America

# Table of Contents

# Polar Bears

**Polar bears** (POH-ler BAYRZ) are the biggest and strongest animals in the snowy **Arctic** (ARK-tik). On four legs, a polar bear is about four feet high. On two legs, a male polar bear might be eleven feet tall. He weighs about 1,500 pounds.

Polar bears are so big and strong that they don't need to live together for protection or for help in getting food. So they usually live alone. They move from place to place as they hunt for food. Such big animals need a lot of food.

*Polar bears have big stomachs. This allows them to go for weeks at a time without a meal.*

# A Snowy Home

The Arctic is at the top of the world. You can see where it is if you look at the top of a globe. The sun doesn't shine as strongly in the Arctic as it does in other places. It is so cold that in some spots the snow never melts and no trees can grow.

But spring comes to the edges of the Arctic. For three months every year, flowers bloom, birds build nests, and animals like polar bears get ready to have families.

*It is cold and snowy most of the year in the Arctic.* ▶

# A Long Winter's Nap

After male and female polar bears **mate** (MAYT), babies can start growing inside the females. The mother bears eat a lot of food. The food is saved as fat. The bear's body lives off that fat while she **hibernates** (HY-ber-nayts), or naps, through the winter.

Only **pregnant** (PREG-nent) polar bears hibernate. In late October, they dig caves into snowy hills. Heat from the polar bear's body is trapped in the cave by thick snow, making a warm room. The polar bear makes a hole in the ceiling to let in fresh air.

◀ *Polar bears that aren't pregnant hunt all winter long.*

# Bear Bodies

Polar bears are **marine** (mah-REEN) animals. They find much of their food in or near the water. Hollow, oily hairs on top of soft fur help polar bears float. Polar bears have long necks and high rear ends. Their webbed feet make great paddles for swimming. And their big paws make it easy for them to walk in the snow. The fur on the bottom of their paws helps keep them steady on slippery ice.

Non-hibernating polar bears hunt all winter, even in blizzards. Polar bears have stomachs that can store more than 150 pounds of food. So they can go for weeks without eating.

*The skin on a polar bear's paw is black. Dark colors hold heat better, so the dark skin helps keep their paws warm when they walk on snow and ice.*

# What's for Dinner?

Polar bears are hunters. Their white fur makes it easy for them to hide in the snow and catch animals by surprise. Strong jaws and sharp teeth allow them to eat big animals. They often eat seals. But polar bears also eat fish, rabbits, birds, and bird eggs. Polar bears are **omnivores** (AHM-nih-vorz). That means they eat everything! They even eat plants, such as **algae** (AL-jee), moss, and grass.

*Although polar bears are good hunters,* ▶
*the seals that they hunt often get away.*

# The Food Chain

Because polar bears are so big, they are near the top of the Arctic food chain. Algae is at the bottom.

Most of the year, the Arctic ground is frozen or covered with snow. Algae is the plant that grows best in the Arctic. It can grow under the ice when the sun shines through. Algae is eaten by tiny fish called **arthropods** (AR-throw-podz). These little fish become food for a bigger fish, the Arctic cod. The cod is food for almost all of the bigger Arctic animals, such as seals, walruses, whales, and polar bears.

*All of the animals in the Arctic, from the polar bear to the great humpback whale, depend on algae for food.*

17

# Great White Hunters

Polar bears spend much of their time hunting for food. In the spring, the ice on the water breaks up. Polar bears use the pieces of ice as boats to ride while hunting seals. They dive into the water to surprise the seals. They close their noses and open their eyes under water.

On top of the ice, polar bears hide in the snow. They crawl like cats. They cover their black noses with their paws or hide them under snow. Polar bears sometimes wait by breaks in the ice where seals come up for air, like cats waiting by mouse holes.

*Polar bears paddle with their front legs and* ▸
*steer with their back legs when they swim.*
*They can swim for many hours at a time.*

# Bears Helping People

The **Inuit** (IN-yoo-it) people are some-times called **Eskimos** (ES-kih-mohz). These Arctic people have lived beside polar bears for hundreds of years. Like polar bears, the Inuit of long ago had to hunt to survive. They watched polar bears and copied the bears' hunting tricks.

After Inuit hunters killed an animal, they thanked it for becoming food and clothes. They showed their thanks by using almost every part of the bear's body. The meat was eaten, and the fur became clothing. But the bones were never used or harmed. The Inuit believed that this let the animals be born again.

◄ *The Inuit depend on the animals of the Arctic to help them survive in very cold weather.*

# People Helping Bears

Today, people are the polar bears' worst enemies. People who want Arctic oil for **fuel** (FYOOL) have ruined parts of the polar bears' home by digging for oil. Hunters have killed polar bears for **trophies** (TRO-feez). Other people worry that polar bears will disappear forever. The five Arctic countries, Canada, Greenland, Norway, Russia, and the United States, passed a law in 1967 to protect polar bear mothers and cubs. Thanks to that law, there are now between 20,000 and 40,000 polar bears living in the Arctic.

# Glossary

**algae** (AL-jee)  A water plant with no roots, stems, or leaves.

**Arctic** (ARK-tik)  The area of land and water at or near the North Pole.

**arthropod** (AR-throw-pod)  A creature with a shell but no backbone.

**Eskimos** (ES-kih-mohz)  Another name for the Inuit people.

**fuel** (FYOOL)  Something used to make energy, warmth, or power.

**hibernate** (HY-ber-nayt)  To spend the winter sleeping.

**Inuit** (IN-yoo-it)  American Indian person or people whose homeland is the Arctic.

**marine** (mah-REEN)  Living in or near the water.

**mate** (MAYT)  A special joining of male and female bodies. After mating, the female may become pregnant.

**omnivores** (AHM-nih-vorz)  An animal that eats both animals and plants.

**polar bear** (POH-ler BAYR)  Great white bear that lives in the Arctic.

**pregnant** (PREG-nent)  When a female animal has an unborn baby growing inside her body.

**trophy** (TRO-fee)  A prize usually given when someone defeats someone or something.

# Index